Overheard
in America

New York • Miami • Chicago • Los Angeles

Overheard IN America

Judith Henry

ATRIA BOOKS

New York London Toronto Sydney

To
Molly, Annabelle, Avi, & Tessa

ATRIA BOOKS

1230 Avenue of the Americas
New York, NY 10020

ISBN-13: 978-0-7432-8797-5
ISBN-10:   0-7432-8797-5

First Atria Books hardcover edition October 2006

10 9 8 7 6 5 4 3 2 1

ATRIA B O O K S is a trademark of Simon & Schuster, Inc.

Printed in China by South China Printing Co.Ltd.

For information regarding special discounts for bulk
purchases, please contact Simon & Schuster Special Sales
at 1-800-456-6798 or business@simonandschuster.com.

Introduction

"Her personality makes her prettier." I heard that sentence in a crowded elevator shortly after moving to New York. I paused and repeated the sentence to myself. I liked both the sound of the words and the sentiment, so I reached in my bag for a pen and paper while repeating the sentence over and over as a mantra. I often repeat a sentence until I am able to record it: "I'm thirty fuckin' years old already, ya know. I'm thirty fuckin' years old already, ya know. I'm thirty fuckin' years old already, ya know."

I've been called an eavesdropper, but I don't listen in on entire conversations. What I find interesting is sentences taken out of context. I heard in a Japanese restaurant: "Did I tell you about the time my boss bit me?" And while standing on the platform waiting for my train, I heard the man next to me declare, "Just think what I could have done without her!"

I grew up in suburban Ohio and moved to New York City as soon as I finished college. The chaos and diversity of the city thrills me and I don't go anywhere without a notebook, pen, and camera. In this city, there are no secrets: I often hear the most intimate and personal information on a crowded subway, elevator, or street corner while waiting for the light to change.

With a blend of photography and typography, I document the movement and daily chatter of New Yorkers. For me the essence of a city is its people, and since cities, like people, are unique, after years of concentrating on New York, I took my camera and notebook and began to explore other places.

I started with Los Angeles because I visit there often and appreciate it's quirkiness. I love all the ways it is different from New York. The weather is gorgeous and gardeners seem to be always tending to something. Even though the population is as ethnically diverse as New York, Los Angeles sprawls and people live, work, and congregate in areas separated by many miles. In New York, I just leave home and I'm instantly part of a crowd, but to find people in L.A. one must travel by car like an Angeleno, in traffic and on freeways and always trying to find a place to park.

After I had gathered material from New York and L.A., the East coast and West coast of America, I decided to go north to Chicago, and south to Miami. I wanted to discover for myself, as I always have, what the pulse of discourse on the streets of America sounds and looks like.

Miami was exotic; I knew that! I remembered the flamboyance and brillance, the beat and heat of *Miami Vice*. Little Elian Gonzalez flashed though my mind as I recalled the international custody battle between his Miami family and his Cuban father. I was eager to practice my Spanish and experience the Latino flavor of the city. As I expected, the city was glitz and glamour, sunshine and beach. There is a large Cuban community and also Latinos from Central and South American countries; Spanish is spoken everywhere. Miami is definitely hot!

I'll admit I was skeptical about Chicago! It is the Midwest and therefore I was prejudiced! But the place was impelling; streets are wide and the city's majestic architecture is visible everywhere. Even though I am a people watcher, the towering architecture, somehow always present, competed for my attention. It was easy to navigate by subway and bus, and I was relieved not to have to once park a car. Chicago had great spirit and wasn't at all like the vapid Midwest I experienced in my childhood.

I wasn't surprised to find McDonald's, Starbucks, and a dozen other ubiquitous chains in all four cities, nor was I surprised that fashion and idiom and a general twenty-first-century anxiety is pervasive. Young people everywhere talk the same talk, walk the same walk, dress in similar ways, and decorate their bodies with tatoos and piercings. But as I got caught up in the flux of everyday life, the individual character of each city captivated me. The people I encountered were both alien and totally familiar. In the everyday banter of Americans, I found a rich trove of wisdom, inspiration, and humor.

So, here then is *Overheard in America*: quick glimpses and fragments of talk on the streets, a record of my travels. The book is a sketch, not a portrait, of these cities and I know that there is as much of me here as there is of New York, Miami, Chicago, and Los Angeles.

—J.H.

... 172 Manhattan. **212 923-2714**	
89................. **212 427-7155**	
36.................... **212 876-9041**	
@Charles St..... **212 352-2245**	
314 E 104............ **212 369-5004**	
8 Av................ **212 581-9232**	
W 143.............. **212 694-4837**	
.... **212 243-6206**	
.... **212 942-9625**	

... of The Americas
.... **212 944-2498**
45 E 14............ **212 477-2301**
Av.................. **212 533-1073**
6.................. **212 996-1208**
nt Manhattan..... **212 283-1662**
.... **212 410-7365**

z Insurance
isades Blvd Fort Lee NJ
Manhattan TelNo-**212 876-4864**

z Insurance
.... **212 809-6663**

z Insurance
.... **212 809-8246**
40.................. **212 690-2332**
.... **212 961-9481**
lumbus Av.......... **212 932-1857**

v @W 190th St. **212 795-4475**

anhattan........... **212 679-3318**
4 Park Av S...... **212 679-3318**

Mika Inatome Custom Bridals
11 Worth @Hudson St............ **212 966-7777**
Mika Maria 85 1 Av.................. **212 677-0464**
Mika Overseas Corp
276 5 Av @E 29th St.............. **212 679-6122**
Fax Number...................... **212 679-5150**
Mika Ren 292 W 92............ **212 877-0025**
Stella 306 E 8.................. **212 260-6975**
Mikado Realty Co 135-30 Roosevelt Ave
Flus.............. Manhattan TelNo-**212 594-8000**
Mikados Inc
1017 6 Av @W 38th St.............. **212 871-2010**
Mikaelian Richard DDS
133 E 58 @Lexington Ave............ **212 752-1898**
Mikaelian Sam 245 E 40............ **212 867-2420**
Mikaelians Jewelry Inc
36 W 47 @5th Ave.................. **212 382-0130**
Mikajiri Tomohiro 180 Riverside Blvd
Manhattan....................... **917 441-3901**
Mikala Karen
13 W 120 Manhattan............ **212 828-0049**
Mikalis Jordan 78 Manhattan Av. **212 665-3999**
Mikaliunas Eileen
45 East End Av.................. **212 628-6574**
Eileen T 45 East End Av............ **212 249-9856**
Mikam Graphics
366 N Broadway Jrcho.............. **212 942-4290**
Mikam Graphics Inc
232 Madison Av @E 37th St........ **212 684-9393**
Mikami Akira 343 E 30............ **212 889-6513**
Kuni 400 W 43.................. **212 967-8038**
Masato 304 E 62.................. **646 497-0301**
Maya 250 W 100 Manhattan..... **212 280-6344**
Seiko 34 8 Av................. **212 934-0845**

He said New York but he's really from New Jersey

My life is bogged down with this chronic shopping

I'm quitting
therapy
and starting
acupuncture

I an
peop
acting

n sick and tired of
le strutting around
successful

I'm trying

to have a life!

I'm not attacking
your liberalism,
John

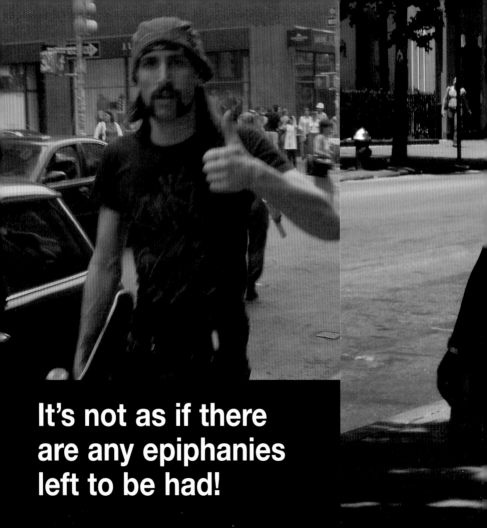

It's not as if there
are any epiphanies
left to be had!

Try to be prettier than you are

Didn't junk happen between us?

I am so late that I never show up

I need to be
with someone
who thinks I'm
the greatest

She may be quiet but she talks too much

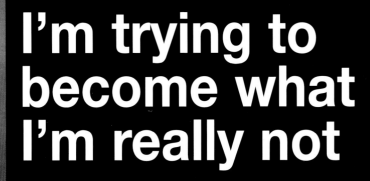

I'm trying to become what I'm really not

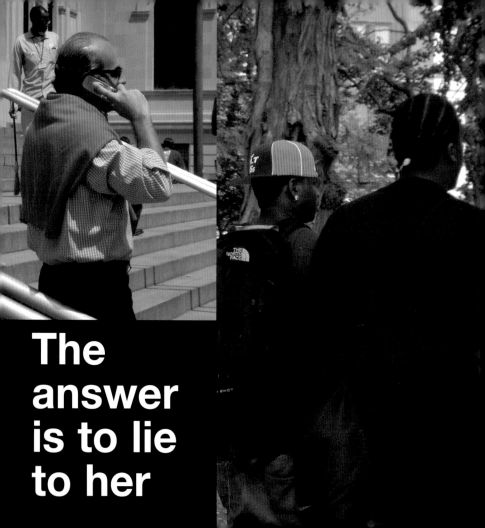

The
answer
is to lie
to her

**What?
MY depression
is depressing
YOU?**

Not
gossip . . .

I'll tell you what the difference is: MONEY!

You have no idea
how much I have
to consider

My travel
agent died—
I don't know
where to go
anymore

He's OK but on the phone he's perfect!

Because he'd rather wallow in it

Maybe you should get yourself a third husband

They think fashion
is about fashion

Nobody's any happier than you if that's any consolation!

It's
YOUR
number
one
priority,
not MY
number
one
priority

I don't NOT care,
I just DON'T care!

If only Derek didn't exist

**In two and a half years
she left him three times**

No	305 624-0064
h	305 691-0940
......	305 644-0742
......	305 261-1900
......	305 631-8213
a	305 756-1904
Hialeah	305 821-3174
......	305 836-9862
Opa Locka ...	305 623-1054
t Mia	305 971-5340
a	305 324-0521
a	305 859-8535
leah	305 885-8062
aleah	305 827-1151
r Aventura ...	305 466-0015
a	305 388-3018
th	305 820-0044
......	305 385-8895
Locka	305 685-2701
n Dr	305 552-5096
RR Miami ...	305 545-5674
......	305 887-6104
t	305 221-0756
SW 26th St...	305 553-3565
mi Beach ...	305 861-8010
al Gables ...	305 774-1579
Miami	305 654-0772
......	305 754-6281
e	305 860-5153
leah	305 231-9696
y	305 372-1350
a	305 644-9524
E 3rd Ct Mia	305 249-9580
......	305 325-8299

Teresita 1134 SW 4th St	305 326-818
Tesla 1088 SW 135th Pl Mia	305 220-469
Tinna 10421 SW 87th Ct Mia	305 598-444
Tirso 9860 SW 48th St Mia	305 595-492
Tibo A 7131 SW 2nd St Mia	305 541-700
Tom 12320 SW 100th Av	305 233-469
Tomas 14536 NE 2nd Ct	305 892-638
Trinidad 1502 NW 30th St	305 636-263
Trinidad 2635 SW 78th Av Mia	305 262-411
Trino 11825 SW 186th St Mia	305 971-221
Valentin	305 232-411
Valentin J 10421 SW 87th Ct Mia	305 273-034
Valerie 1838 NW 15th St Mia	305 324-031
Vanessa 300 74th St Miami Beach ...	305 865-165
Vanessa 2847 NW 93rd St Mia	305 691-642
Vanessa 2935 NW 93rd Sr Mia	305 835-88
Velia 2695 SW 28th Av	305 446-971
Veronica 750 NE 62nd St Mia	305 756-279
Veronica 11701 SW 104th Ct Mia	305 235-544
Veronica 9106 SW 203rd Ter Mia	786 573-17
Vicente 1790 NW 3rd St Mia	305 689-84
Victor 560 NE 34th St Mia	305 572-14
Victor 18133 SW 113th Ct Mia	305 256-78
Victor E 10770 NW 66th St	305 477-74
Victor E 13401 SW 53rd St	305 551-11
Victor M 8828 SW 151st Ct	305 385-03
Victoria 1460 W 43rd Pl Hialeah	305 557-31
Vilma 11470 SW 58th Ter Mia	305 274-28
Violeta 3300 S Dixie Hwy	305 461-31
Virginio 305 W 68th St Hlh	305 823-83
Viviana 7749 SW 88th St Mia	305 596-25
Walter 15622 SW 74th Pl	305 232-23
Wilfredo	
4050 NW 135th St Opa Locka	305 687-67
Wilfredo 2949 NW 92nd St	305 836-44
Wilfredo 170 W 26th St Hialeah	305 863-77
Willy L 8500 Biscayne Blvd El Portal ...	305 757-06
Ximena C 800 N Miami Av Mia	786 316-01

Miami

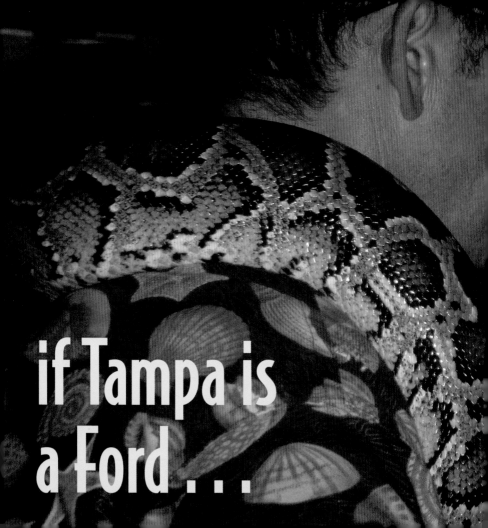

if Tampa is
a Ford . . .

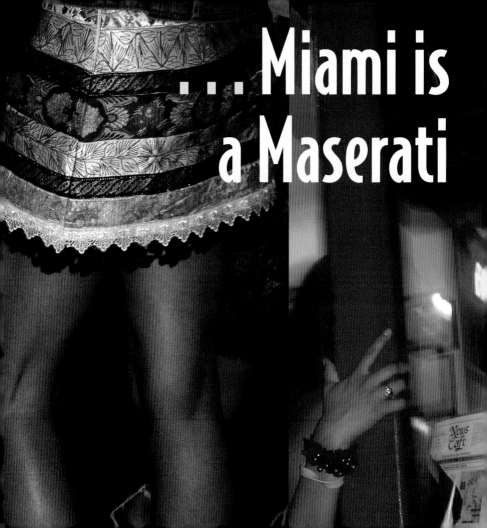

... Miami is
a Maserati

She's the queen of cheating and lying about it

I'll never
change my
212 for
a 305

Isn't mine the most natural you've ever seen?

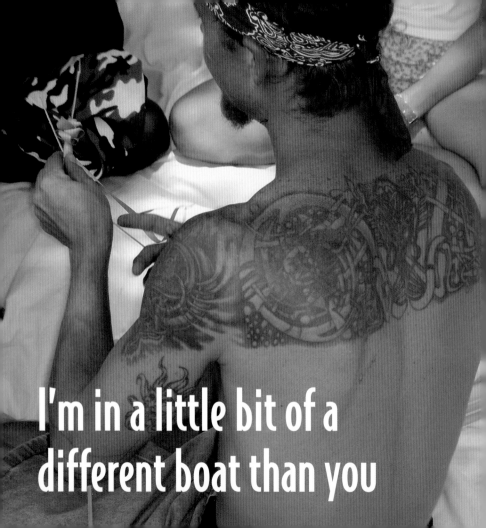

I'm in a little bit of a
different boat than you

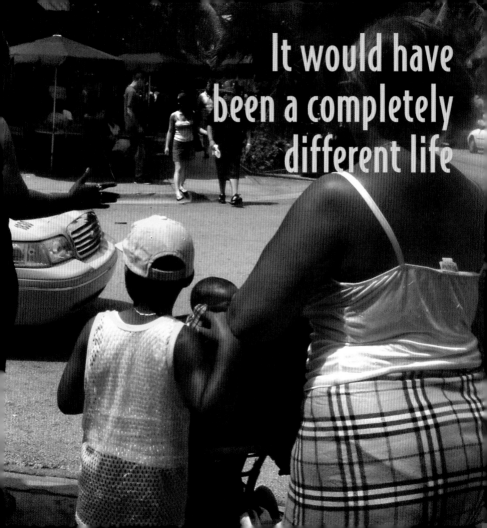

It would have been a completely different life

I'm the last person to talk about politics

She keeps taking pills
but it just hurts worse

For me everything always just works out

I don't want to ever get married but I want a rock

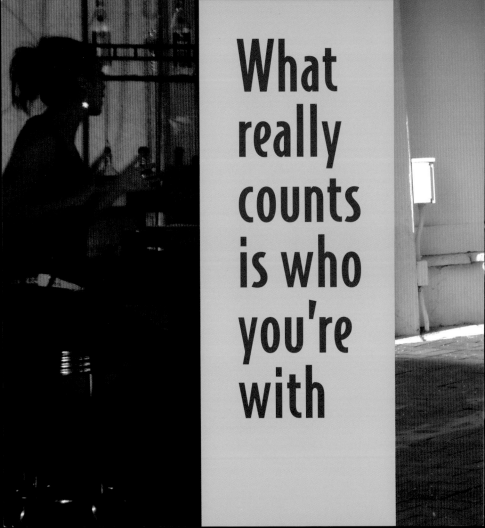

Para mí
la vida es
random

It's a
whole
area that
needs
to be
exploited

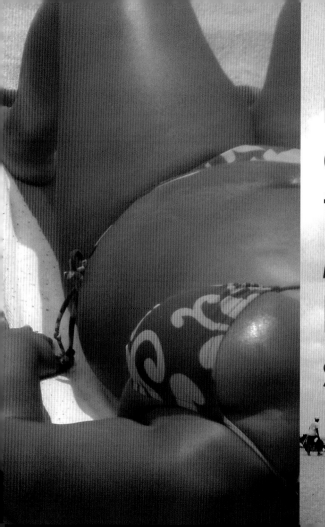

My neighbor came back from Argentina half her size

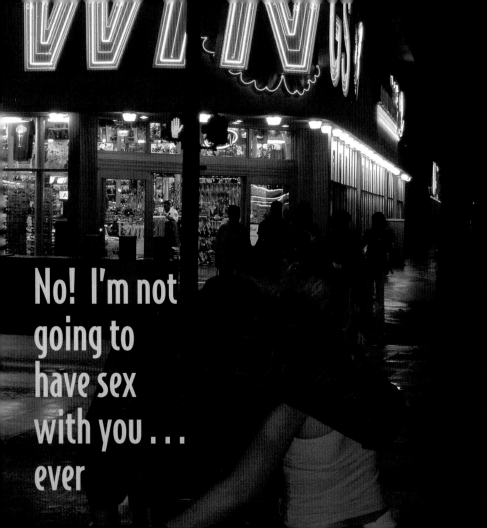

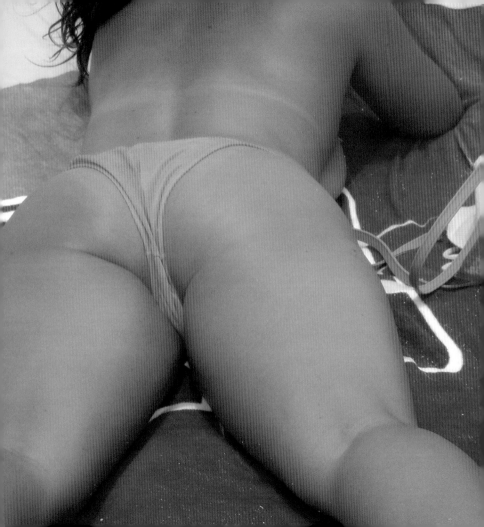

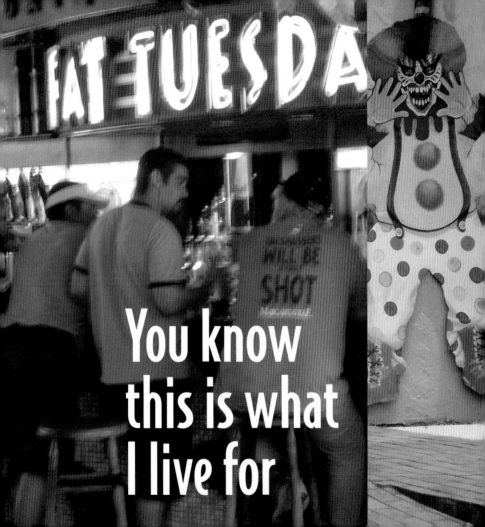

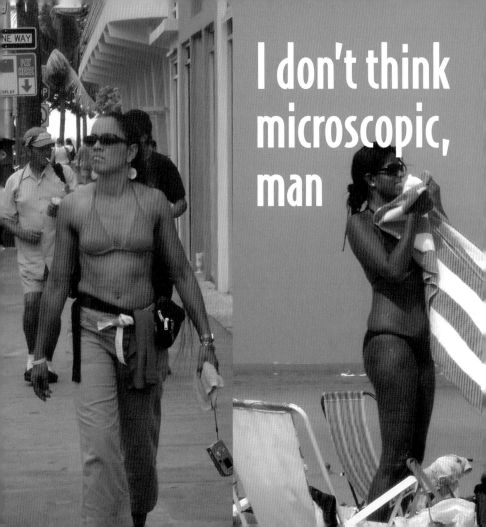

Mañana trabajamos

ALL YOU NEED TO REACH THE BE

We've been in the suburbs for too long

But, I pick at my cuticles

I just lie here and watch the sweat come outta my pores

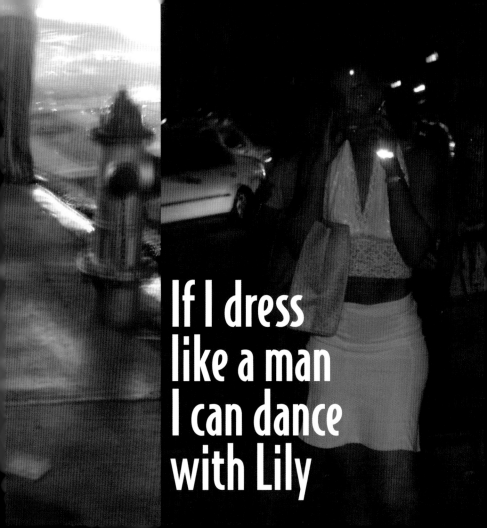

If I dress
like a man
I can dance
with Lily

I done absolutely nothin' wrong!

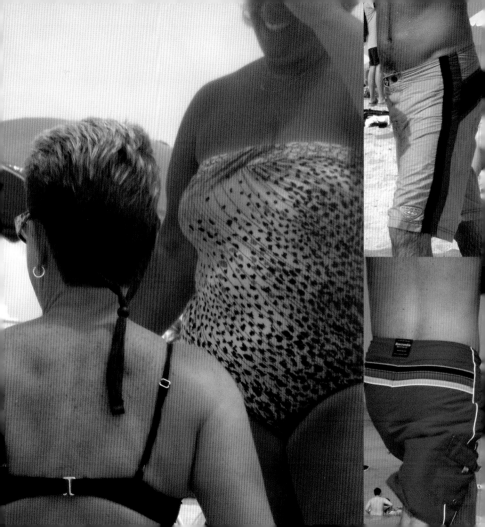

I work, man, but . . .

... I'm on vacation!

Casas de millonarios aburridos

That's how big we're gonna become— BIGGER than Vegas!

Kent W 1555 N Dearborn Pkwy ---- 312 440-0722

Scharringhausen Rexall Drugs

110 Main St Pk Rdg

Toll Free For Enterprise Calls Call Oor Ask
For ---------------------------------- Enterprise-2506
SCHART Eleanore 5029 N Nottingham Av 775-2960
SCHARTZ Steven 395 W Fullerton Pkwy 935-3869
SCHARVER Christopher S

2425 N Janssen Av ---------------------- 528-2521
SCHASSBURGER Wilhelm M

3111 S Normandy Av -------------------- 586-7011
SCHATAN Josh R 1712 N Wood ---------- 486-9138
SCHATELL Riki 6033 N Sheridan Rd ------ 728-7281
SCHATMER John 1636 W Beach Av -------- 278-1399
SCHATT Michael 1322 S Prairie Av -- 312 945-3442
   Michael 1347 E 56th -------------------- 924-0224
SCHATTE June M 7529 W Carmen Av

------------------------------------ 708 867-7615

SCHATTENBERG Eugene D

3627 W 68th Pl --------------------------- 582-9419
SCHATTERBECK Elizabeth

6379 W 78th Av ---------------------------- 631-1587
SCHATTKE Robt 1532 W Birchwood Av -- 274-4003
SCHATTNER Robt R 1338 W Diversey Pkwy

-- 348-9947
SCHATZ A 3440 N Lake Shore Dr --------- 248-6447
   A 7745 S Kedzie Av ---------------------- 737-6948
   Anthony 1850 N Clark ------------- 312 587-1974
   Barry 2145 N Clark --------------------- 327-6595
SCHATZ Barry A PC 161 N Clark --- 312 782-3456
SCHATZ Eileen 550 W Surf -------------- 549-1651
   Eleanor B 3960 N Lake Shore Drive West 871-9910
   J C 7111 N Oketo Av -------------------- 763-5010
   Jim 7111 N Oketo Av -------------------- 763-5427

Chicago

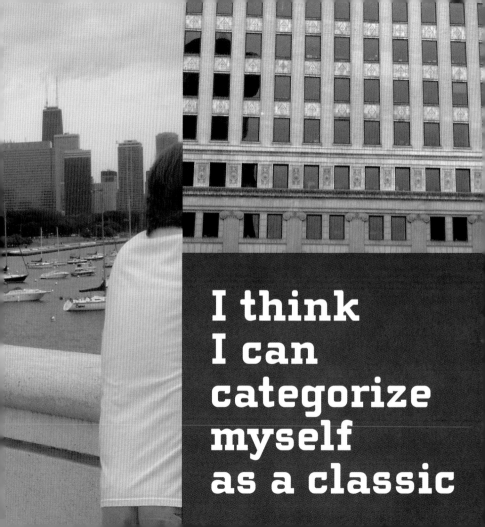

I think
I can
categorize
myself
as a classic

He left me
emotionally
exhausted

Twelve hours in Cleveland is like a lifetime

I ain't never gonna be able to feel good

What do you think, should we go for hot dogs or sushi?

POP CORN

23
S

Today's a fluke— don't get used to it

This whole Ozzie and Harriet fantasy is very real

I don't have a cold;
this is the way I look
without makeup

You and Dad have those small-town blinders on

I sorta dated him before he sorta dated Alice and I sorta dated Marco

I met him at
Weight Watchers

That Britney Spears perfume was overwhelming

Let's get drunk and be someone

Just a margarita or two and I'll be able to go back to work

Yep, I'm the guy who's so politically incorrect

I was feeling
kinda fancy
pants

I bumped into my ex with your ex this morning

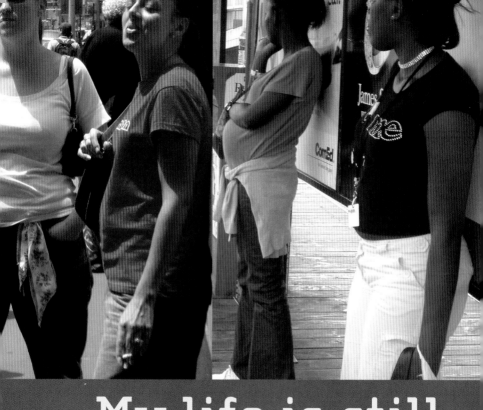

My life is still
way boring

He's married but he's not a grown-up

I prefer to
be invisible

You don't have to tell everybody everything

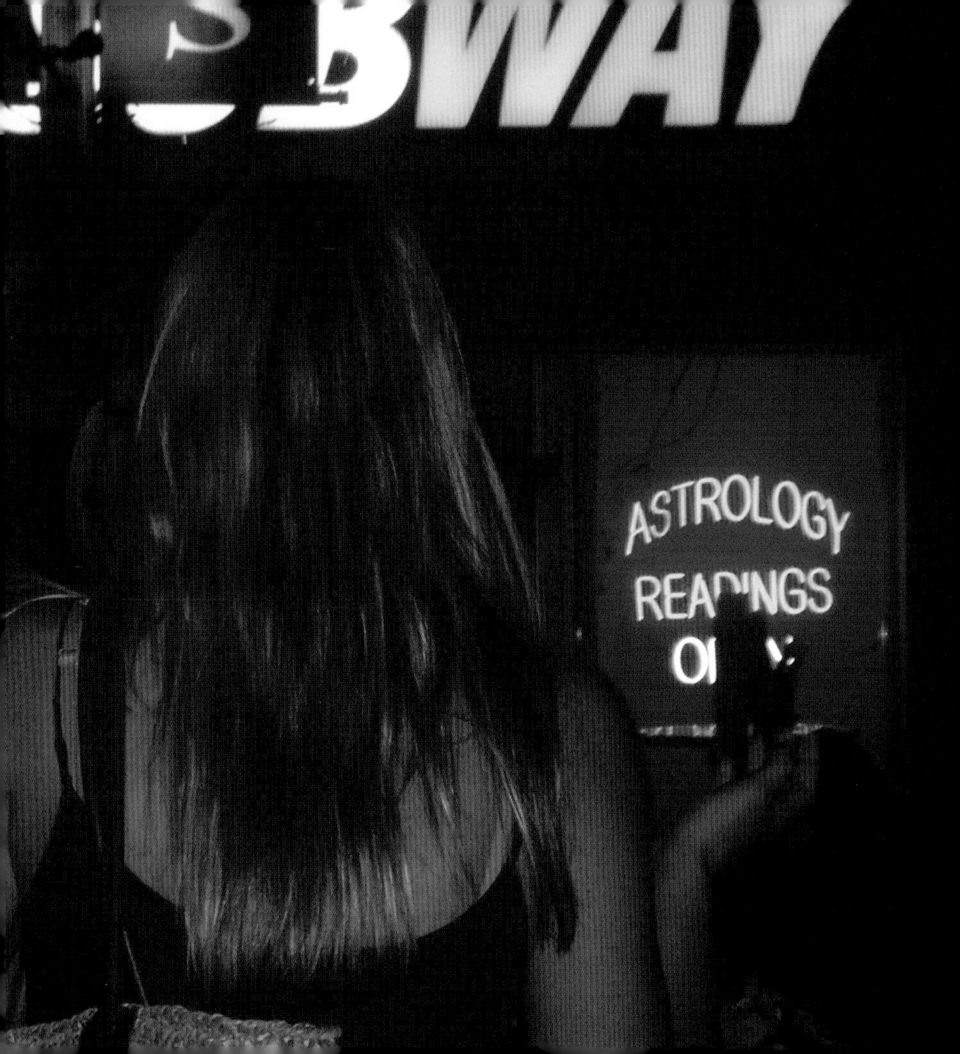
ASTROLOGY

Did you find out any stuff about me?

And he's acting
like I'm faking it

So, Chicago? Could be anywhere

785-9177	19315 Redbridge Ln Tarzana
453-1012	Susan 8384 Equinox Cr Culver City
559-2044	Tamara & John 1174 Amherst Av WL
Corp	Thomas F 535 Pier Av SM
828-4633	BERGAL Bernard 1122 Indiana Av Ven
204-1397	T
818 385-1719	BERGAMIN Claudio BA
474-6123	BERGAMO M L
	Pierpaolo 1720 Pacific Ave Ven
207-0000	BERGAMOT Books 2525 Mich Av SM
	BERGAMOT Cafe 2525 Mich Av SM
818 343-5511	BERGAMOT Station 2525 Mich Av SM
207-6723	BERGAN Ronald D 303 Ocean Av SM
914-9243	BERGANZA David
	3345 Cattaraugus Av Culver City
275-1601	BERGATWO Leonard
818 343-8533	BERGE Fay
	Raul Ricardo
442-0333	BERGELSON Gordon
818 609-1151	L A
275-1949	BERGELSON N WHwd
	BERGEN Bannister 12460 Culver Blvd LA
284-8141	Barbara H WLA
312-3990	Daniel CC

Los Angeles

The Ivy

Valet
Parking
$3.50 With Thanks

Operated by:
Pyramid Parking, Inc.
(888) 80-Pyramid

Well, you
know in this
town we do
stuff!

I beg you, get over yourself already

Most of
the time
I resent
people
with
talent

She used to be
someone else

That's
why I
look as
good
as I do

Talent has nothing to do with success in this world!

What was that—
a sudden wave
of morality?

Ya wanna be successful— stop trying to be loved!

You moved out here to look COOL?

Ya gotta
live in the
real world

Beware of the neo-puritans!

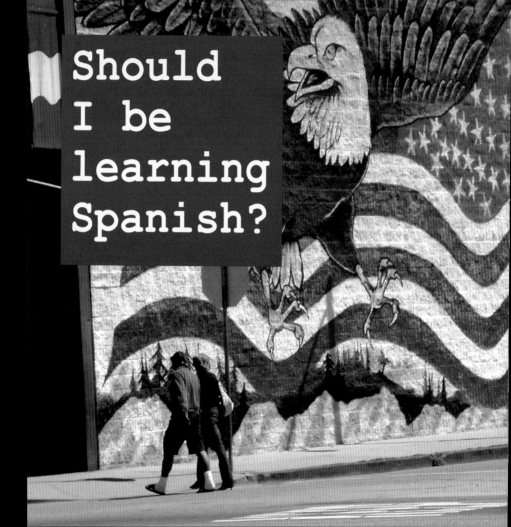

Should
I be
learning
Spanish?

PAINT & BODY

Is he a boob freak?

If I know
anything I
know film

Do you have an agent?

So your mother's
a lesbian, right?

But I didn't tell you the worst part yet!

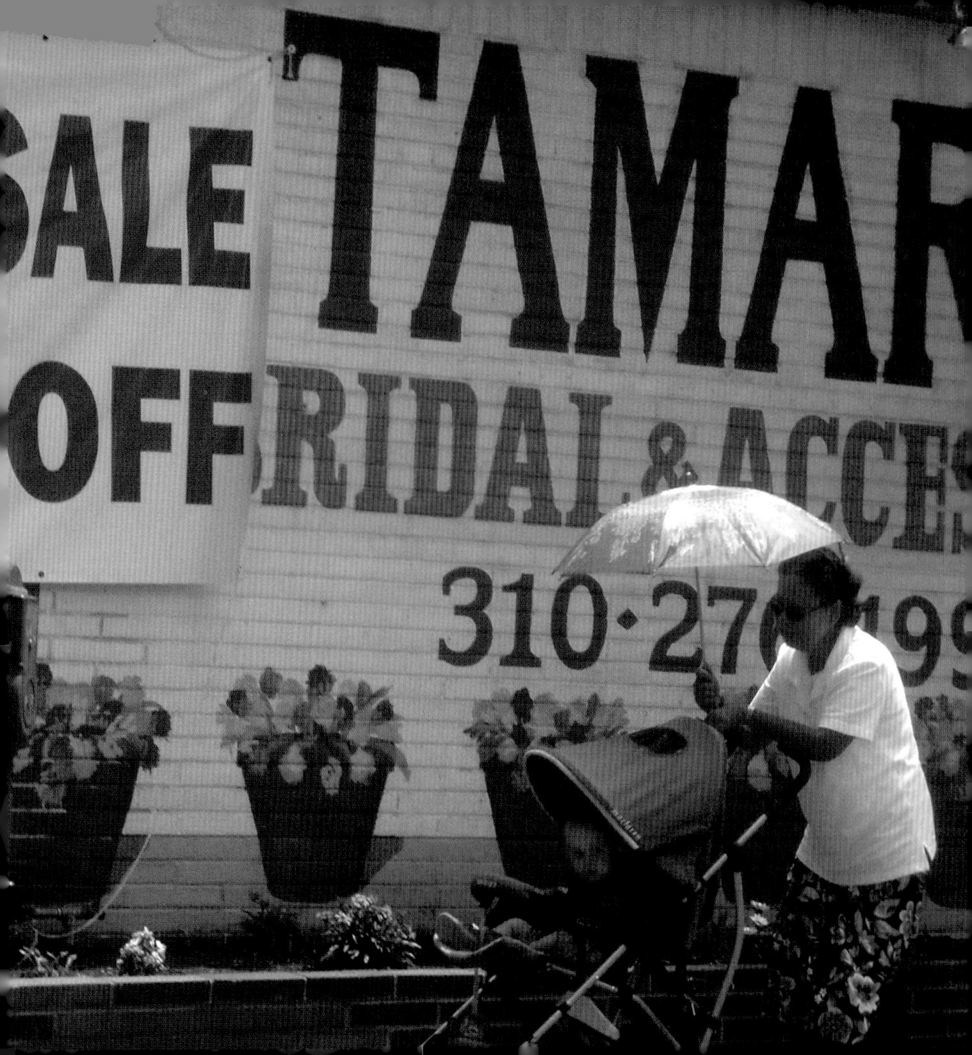
SALE
OFF
TAMAR
RIDAL & ACCES
310·27

I finally learned
to levitate

I'm pretty good
at action scenes

She was thrilled
with her deceit

Does it go in your belly button or next to it?

My sex
drive is
so low
I have
to fake
orgasm
with
myself

Does it involve money?

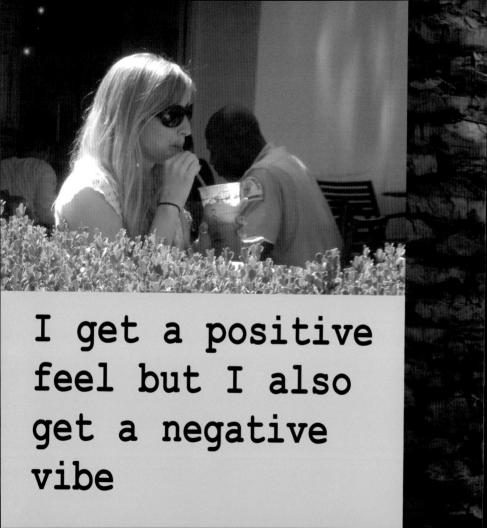

She has good eyesight
but it's not like
hindsight!

Nothing's ever movin' fast enough

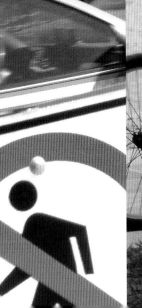

I started
in New York
and have
gone
downhill
ever since